# Lead Like Moses
## Ten Characteristics of Good Leaders

Ken Hensley

# LEAD LIKE MOSES
## INTRODUCTION

---

Although I have been a pastor for nearly twenty-five years, I still remember the first Bible class I was ever asked to teach. It was a Wednesday night class for three and four year-olds at the church I grew up in. My friend, Wally, and I were recruited (or volunteered, I honestly don't remember) to teach a thirteen-week class on famous Old Testament characters. These were the all-stars of the Old Testament: Abraham, Joseph, Noah, Moses, and David, among others.

After the first night, when much of our time and energy was spent on crowd control (a losing battle), Wally looked at me and asked, "What if we screw this up? What if we accidently tell them that Moses built the ark and they live the rest of their lives believing Moses actually built the ark instead of Noah?"

"You mean Moses didn't build the ark?"

We both laughed but with an immediate awareness of our obligation to tell the stories accurately. We knew it was unlikely that any of the kids would remember either of us; but we both hoped they would remember the faith of Abraham and the courage of Esther.

Those characters have found their way into many of my sermons and classes. As a leader, I have found myself returning to one story in particular: the story of Moses. This godly man is a living picture of the kind of leader God is looking for. Far from perfect, Moses begins like many of us do (reluctantly), stumbles along the way, and tries to finish well.

What you have in your hands is a short workbook that I have used with small groups and large classes. It is designed to

# LEAD LIKE MOSES

distill ten characteristics of leadership in a way that provokes discussion and leads to action. I would recommend you process this material with a group of people, learning from each other's experiences and holding each other accountable to be the best leaders you are capable of being.

May each of us live to see Moses' prayer answered in our own lives: *"May the favor of the Lord our God rest upon us; establish the work of our hands for us — yes, establish the work of our hands" (Psalm 90).*

Ken Hensley
Highlands Ranch, CO

# LEAD LIKE MOSES
## TABLE OF CONTENTS

# Lead Like Moses
## Chapter One: An Introduction to Moses

---

**Main Point: Moses is a good model for what God expects from spiritual leaders.**

Of the 66 books in the Bible, Moses is mentioned in 32 of them. When Moses came into leadership, the Hebrews had been in Egypt for 430 years and had grown to over 2 million people.

Moses' task: To lead a group of people that he did not want to lead in a task for which he had never volunteered.

What would the timeline of your leadership journey look like? For most of us, it would look something like this:

Our leadership chart would be a mixture of ups and downs, wins and losses. Even the best leaders would have moments they'd like to go back and do over.

Moses was no different. As we study the life of Moses, we'll notice the dips and swings in his leadership. It's not the absence of difficult times (or bad decisions) that make for a great leader; it's how they respond to those times.

✛ **What would be one of your leadership "do-overs"?**

---

# LEAD LIKE MOSES

_____

_____

_____

_____

## The Life of Moses: Act One

Moses was born to Jewish parents at a time when the Hebrews were persecuted.

_As the time drew near for God to fulfill his promise to Abraham, the number of our people in Egypt had greatly increased. Then 'a new king, to whom Joseph meant nothing, came to power in Egypt.' He dealt treacherously with our people and oppressed our ancestors by forcing them to throw out their newborn babies so that they would die. "At that time Moses was born, and he was no ordinary child. For three months he was cared for by his family. When he was placed outside, Pharaoh's daughter took him and brought him up as her own son. Moses was educated in all the wisdom of the Egyptians and was powerful in speech and action._ – Acts 7:17-22

Moses is born into persecution and raised in privilege. Here is what the late John Stott had to say about this passage:

> The Israelites' exile and slavery in Egypt lasted for four bitter centuries. Had God forgotten his people, and his promise to bless them? No. He had warned Abraham of their 400 years of enslavement and mistreatment ... It was _at that time_, when the people's sufferings were greatest and their prospects bleakest, that _Moses was born_, their God-appointed deliverer ... For the first _three_

# LEAD LIKE MOSES

> *months* of his life he was nurtured by his own mother, but was then brought up is the Egyptian palace as the adopted son of Pharaoh's daughter. He was thus *educated in all the wisdom of the Egyptians* and became *powerful in speech and action.*[1]

By birth, Moses should have been raised as a slave. Instead, he is raised in privilege in the most powerful household in Egypt.

✚ **How might this experience have uniquely prepared Moses for leadership?**

_____

_____

_____

_____

_____

✚ **What challenges might Moses' upbringing have created?**

_____

_____

_____

_____

_____

---

[1] Stott, John R. W. *The Message of Acts: The Spirit, the Church & the World.* Leicester, England; Downers Grove, IL: InterVarsity Press, 1994. Print. The Bible Speaks Today.

# LEAD LIKE MOSES

## The Life of Moses: Act Two

Before God could use Moses, Moses had to be broken and learn humility. Hans Finzel calls this earning his "BD Degree" – "back of the desert" degree.

*"When Moses was forty years old, he decided to visit his own people, the Israelites. He saw one of them being mistreated by an Egyptian, so he went to his defense and avenged him by killing the Egyptian. Moses thought that his own people would realize that God was using him to rescue them, but they did not. The next day Moses came upon two Israelites who were fighting. He tried to reconcile them by saying, 'Men, you are brothers; why do you want to hurt each other?' "But the man who was mistreating the other pushed Moses aside and said, 'Who made you ruler and judge over us? Are you thinking of killing me as you killed the Egyptian yesterday?' When Moses heard this, he fled to Midian, where he settled as a foreigner and had two sons. – Acts 7:23-29*

✠ **Why would Moses think that this action would help his own people "realize God was using him to rescue them"?**

_____

_____

_____

_____

_____

Instead of being recognized as a rescuer, Moses is accused of acting as ruler and judge. Fearing the consequences of his actions, he flees to Midian and lives as a foreigner.

# LEAD LIKE MOSES

✜ As a leader, when have your actions been misinterpreted?

_____

_____

_____

_____

_____

✜ How many of those were the result of relying on your own timing instead of God's timing?

✜ What did you learn from those experiences?

_____

_____

_____

_____

_____

## The Life of Moses: Act Three

_"After forty years had passed, an angel appeared to Moses in the flames of a burning bush in the desert near Mount Sinai. When he saw this, he was amazed at the sight. As he went over to get a closer look, he heard the Lord say: 'I am the God of your fathers, the God of Abraham, Isaac and Jacob.' Moses trembled with fear_

# LEAD LIKE MOSES

*and did not dare to look. "Then the Lord said to him, 'Take off your sandals, for the place where you are standing is holy ground. I have indeed seen the oppression of my people in Egypt. I have heard their groaning and have come down to set them free. Now come, I will send you back to Egypt.' "This is the same Moses they had rejected with the words, 'Who made you ruler and judge?' He was sent to be their ruler and deliverer by God himself, through the angel who appeared to him in the bush. He led them out of Egypt and performed wonders and signs in Egypt, at the Red Sea and for forty years in the wilderness. "This is the Moses who told the Israelites, 'God will raise up for you a prophet like me from your own people.' He was in the assembly in the wilderness, with the angel who spoke to him on Mount Sinai, and with our ancestors; and he received living words to pass on to us.* – Acts 7:30-38

It was not until Moses hit eighty (80!) that he was ready to lead.

✤ **What do you think had been happening during this time?**

_____

_____

_____

_____

_____

# LEAD LIKE MOSES

❖ How can you improve your ability to learn from desert experiences?

_____

_____

_____

_____

_____

_____

_____

_____

_____

_____

_____

_____

_____

# LEAD LIKE MOSES

## CHAPTER TWO: THE RELUCTANT LEADER

**Main point**: God can use us even when we think we're not ready.

## The Prayer Of A Reluctant Leader

*"Lord, send someone else"* – Exodus 4:13 (Moses responding to God's call)

Even though Moses had been selected by God to lead God's people, Moses still had to accept the task of leadership. Being selected by God does not always lead to enthusiasm or eagerness; in fact, it can often lead to reluctance.

✤ **What have you dreamed of doing but haven't because you felt inadequate or unprepared?**

_____

_____

_____

_____

_____

## Overcoming Objections

What makes today's story so compelling is this: *God can use us even when we think we're not ready to be used.* Before Moses

# LEAD LIKE MOSES

can become a great leader, God has to first overcome his objections.

*Now Moses was tending the flock of Jethro his father-in-law, the priest of Midian, and he led the flock to the far side of the wilderness and came to Horeb, the mountain of God. There the angel of the Lord appeared to him in flames of fire from within a bush. Moses saw that though the bush was on fire it did not burn up. So Moses thought, "I will go over and see this strange sight— why the bush does not burn up." When the Lord saw that he had gone over to look, God called to him from within the bush, "Moses! Moses!" And Moses said, "Here I am." "Do not come any closer," God said. "Take off your sandals, for the place where you are standing is holy ground." Then he said, "I am the God of your father, the God of Abraham, the God of Isaac and the God of Jacob." At this, Moses hid his face, because he was afraid to look at God. The Lord said, "I have indeed seen the misery of my people in Egypt. I have heard them crying out because of their slave drivers, and I am concerned about their suffering. So I have come down to rescue them from the hand of the Egyptians and to bring them up out of that land into a good and spacious land, a land flowing with milk and honey—the home of the Canaanites, Hittites, Amorites, Perizzites, Hivites and Jebusites. And now the cry of the Israelites has reached me, and I have seen the way the Egyptians are oppressing them. So now, go. I am sending you to Pharaoh to bring my people the Israelites out of Egypt." –* Exodus 3:1-10

✚ **What made this ground holy? Why is this important to the story?**

_____

_____

_____

# LEAD LIKE MOSES

_____

_____

✤ **What does the task at hand require?**

_____

_____

_____

_____

The bottom line is this: God's people need a leader and God is asking Moses to be that leader. There will be times when God calls us to accept a challenge we don't feel prepared for.

_But Moses said to God, "Who am I that I should go to Pharaoh and bring the Israelites out of Egypt?" And God said, "I will be with you. And this will be the sign to you that it is I who have sent you: When you have brought the people out of Egypt, you will worship God on this mountain." Moses said to God, "Suppose I go to the Israelites and say to them, 'The God of your fathers has sent me to you,' and they ask me, 'What is his name?' Then what shall I tell them?" God said to Moses, "I am who I am. This is what you are to say to the Israelites: 'I am has sent me to you.'" –_ Exodus 3:11-14

# LEAD LIKE MOSES

✤ **What objections does Moses raise?**

_____

_____

_____

_____

_____

✤ **How does God respond to these objections?**

_____

_____

_____

_____

_____

*God also said to Moses, "Say to the Israelites, 'The Lord, the God of your fathers—the God of Abraham, the God of Isaac and the God of Jacob—has sent me to you.' "This is my name forever, the name you shall call me from generation to generation. "Go, assemble the elders of Israel and say to them, 'The Lord, the God of your fathers—the God of Abraham, Isaac and Jacob— appeared to me and said: I have watched over you and have seen what has been done to you in Egypt. And I have promised to bring you up out of your misery in Egypt into the land of the Canaanites, Hittites, Amorites, Perizzites, Hivites and Jebusites— a land flowing with milk and honey.' "The elders of Israel will listen to you. Then you and the elders are to go to the king of*

# Lead Like Moses

*Egypt and say to him, 'The Lord, the God of the Hebrews, has met with us. Let us take a three-day journey into the wilderness to offer sacrifices to the Lord our God.' But I know that the king of Egypt will not let you go unless a mighty hand compels him. So I will stretch out my hand and strike the Egyptians with all the wonders that I will perform among them. After that, he will let you go. "And I will make the Egyptians favorably disposed toward this people, so that when you leave you will not go empty-handed. Every woman is to ask her neighbor and any woman living in her house for articles of silver and gold and for clothing, which you will put on your sons and daughters. And so you will plunder the Egyptians." – Exodus 3:15-22*

✤ **Why didn't God fire Moses and pick someone else?**

_____

_____

_____

_____

_____

## Keep Your Eyes on God

When God calls you to a task, he is willing to use his *mighty hand* to help you succeed.

There is a saying that says, "Where God guides, God provides."

To be effective, you need to take your eyes off your weaknesses and focus on God's strengths. At some point, you have to move from operating out of doubt to operating out of faith.

# LEAD LIKE MOSES

Remember: A small step of faith is always better than a large step of doubt.

✤ **Is there an area of leadership or opportunity that you are currently reluctant to tackle? If so, what is one step of faith you can take right now?**

_____

_____

_____

_____

_____

_____

_____

_____

_____

_____

# LEAD LIKE MOSES

## CHAPTER THREE: WHAT A LEADER SEES

**Main point:** Effective leaders follow a vision from God.

"A leader is one who sees more than others see, who sees farther than others see, and who sees before others do." – LeRoy Eims

> Vision is rooted in God. God transcends time: He is the God of the past, but repeatedly in Scripture he is the God of the future. We need to fix our attention on who he is and what he wants to do. Theology, in the Scriptures, is not a doctrinal discourse but the record of God's revealing himself through history. We must assume God will continue to reveal himself in the future. We can't, therefore, live only in the past, because God is calling us to something. There's always something out in front of us.[2]

*The Lord said, "I have indeed seen the misery of my people in Egypt. I have heard them crying out because of their slave drivers, and I am concerned about their suffering. So I have come down to rescue them from the hand of the Egyptians and to bring them up out of that land into a good and spacious land, a land flowing with milk and honey—the home of the Canaanites, Hittites, Amorites, Perizzites, Hivites and Jebusites. – Exodus 3:7-8*

---

[2] Anderson, Leith. "Leading Into the Future." *Renewing Your Church through Vision and Planning: 30 Strategies to Transform Your Ministry.* Ed. Marshall Shelley. Vol. 2. Minneapolis, MN: Bethany House, 1997. 70. Print. Library of Leadership Development.

# LEAD LIKE MOSES

✤ **Where does Moses receive his vision?**

_____

_____

_____

_____

_____

✤ **Why is this important for those involved in spiritual leadership?**

_____

_____

_____

_____

_____

## When Do People Need Vision?

**In the beginning ...**

_"Therefore, say to the Israelites: 'I am the Lord, and I will bring you out from under the yoke of the Egyptians. I will free you from being slaves to them, and I will redeem you with an outstretched arm and with mighty acts of judgment. I will take you as my own people, and I will be your God. Then you will know that I am the Lord your God, who brought you out from under the yoke of the Egyptians. And I will bring you to the land I swore with_

# LEAD LIKE MOSES

*uplifted hand to give to Abraham, to Isaac and to Jacob. I will give it to you as a possession. I am the Lord.'"* – Exodus 6:6-8

✤ **Why is vision important at the start of project?**

_____

_____

_____

_____

## In the middle ...

*"I will establish your borders from the Red Sea to the Mediterranean Sea, and from the desert to the Euphrates River. I will give into your hands the people who live in the land, and you will drive them out before you."* – Exodus 23:31

✤ **Why might the middle of a project or season be the most difficult?**

_____

_____

_____

_____

# LEAD LIKE MOSES

✚ **How can you plan for and overcome these obstacles?**

_____

_____

_____

_____

_____

Moses kept the vision of the Promised Land alive for 40 years!

**At the end ...**

*The eternal God is your refuge, and underneath are the everlasting arms. He will drive out your enemies before you, saying, 'Destroy them!' So Israel will live in safety; Jacob will dwell secure in a land of grain and new wine, where the heavens drop dew. Blessed are you, Israel! Who is like you, a people saved by the Lord? He is your shield and helper and your glorious sword. Your enemies will cower before you, and you will tread on their heights."* – Deuteronomy 33:27-29 (the blessing of Moses)

Moses continued to celebrate the vision to the very end.

✚ **What can you do to celebrate the achievement of a vision?**

_____

_____

_____

# LEAD LIKE MOSES

---

---

## Common Vision Obstacles that Spiritual Leaders Face

Read Psalm 106. Here are the obstacles that Moses faced as a leader:

- He was trying to implement a bold plan.
- He didn't have much in common with the people he led.
- He was old and getting older.
- He was unknown.
- Because of his upbringing, there was a cultural gap between him and his followers.
- He was asking people to move out of their comfort zone.
- His followers were constantly whining and complaining.
- He had to deal with strong personalities who opposed him.

✤ **Which of these do you identify with and why?**

---

---

---

---

---

# LEAD LIKE MOSES
## Vision Gets Things Done

*"This is the same Moses they had rejected with the words, 'Who made you ruler and judge?' He was sent to be their ruler and deliverer by God himself, through the angel who appeared to him in the bush. **He led them out** of Egypt and performed wonders and signs in Egypt, at the Red Sea and for forty years in the wilderness."* – Acts 7:35-36

After all was said and done, Moses got the job done – he led them out of Egypt. For vision to be vision, it must be matched with execution. In other words, things get done.

> "Leaders are pioneers. They are people who venture into unexplored territory. They guide us to new and often unfamiliar destinations. People who take the lead are the foot soldiers in the campaigns for change. The unique reason for having leaders – their differentiating function – is to move us forward. Leaders get us going someplace." – Posner and Kouzes, The Leadership Challenge

# LEAD LIKE MOSES

## CHAPTER FOUR: BECOMING AN OPTIMISTIC LEADER

---

**Main point:** The people around you need you to be an optimistic leader.

The people you lead are desperate for hope. They need to believe that there is a greater good they can accomplish together than by going it alone. They will be tempted to quit when plans fail or obstacles are encountered. They need you to be an optimistic leader.

✤ **In your life, who are the people who need you to be an optimistic leader?**

_____

_____

_____

_____

_____

## What Kind of Leader will You Be?

Optimism is more than positive thinking. As today's story illustrates, the good news is that our optimism is rooted in the trustworthiness of God.

# LEAD LIKE MOSES

*When Pharaoh let the people go, God did not lead them on the road through the Philistine country, though that was shorter. For God said, "If they face war, they might change their minds and return to Egypt." So God led the people around by the desert road toward the Red Sea. The Israelites went up out of Egypt ready for battle.* – Exodus 13:17-18

No definitive documentation of Philistine military strength at the time of the exodus has survived from the ancient world. We know, however, that the Philistines were so daunting a fighting force at the time of the conquest, forty years later and beyond, that even at Joshua's death their territory remained unconquered (cf. Josh 13:1–5). We also know that they were bold enough to attack Egypt proper in an effort to capture territory in the days of Ramses III, that is, about 1188 bc, suggesting that they considered themselves at that time—considerably after the Israelites had entered Canaan—potentially able to defeat even the Egyptians, depending on the circumstances.[3]

✙ **Why doesn't God send them on the shorter route?**

_____

_____

_____

_____

_____

---

[3] Stuart, Douglas K. *Exodus*. Vol. 2. Nashville: Broadman & Holman Publishers, 2006. Print. The New American Commentary.

# LEAD LIKE MOSES

✜ **What does God understand about leadership development (and human development in general)?**

_____

_____

_____

_____

_____

## A Leadership Test

*Then the Lord said to Moses, "Tell the Israelites to turn back and encamp near Pi Hahiroth, between Migdol and the sea. They are to encamp by the sea, directly opposite Baal Zephon. Pharaoh will think, 'The Israelites are wandering around the land in confusion, hemmed in by the desert.' And I will harden Pharaoh's heart, and he will pursue them. But I will gain glory for myself through Pharaoh and all his army, and the Egyptians will know that I am the Lord." So the Israelites did this. When the king of Egypt was told that the people had fled, Pharaoh and his officials changed their minds about them and said, "What have we done? We have let the Israelites go and have lost their services!" So he had his chariot made ready and took his army with him. He took six hundred of the best chariots, along with all the other chariots of Egypt, with officers over all of them. The Lord hardened the heart of Pharaoh king of Egypt, so that he pursued the Israelites, who were marching out boldly. The Egyptians—all Pharaoh's horses and chariots, horsemen and troops—pursued the Israelites and overtook them as they camped by the sea near Pi Hahiroth, opposite Baal Zephon. As Pharaoh approached, the Israelites looked up, and there were the Egyptians, marching after them. They were terrified and cried out to the Lord. They*

# LEAD LIKE MOSES

*said to Moses, "Was it because there were no graves in Egypt that you brought us to the desert to die? What have you done to us by bringing us out of Egypt? Didn't we say to you in Egypt, 'Leave us alone; let us serve the Egyptians'? It would have been better for us to serve the Egyptians than to die in the desert!" –* Exodus 14:1-12

Moses faces two specific challenges:

- Will he be led by popular opinion or will he be the leader?
- Will he adopt the negative influences around him or be a positive leader?

✛ **What is the danger of a leader simply following popular opinion?**

_____

_____

_____

_____

_____

✛ **Why are negative influences sometimes so attractive?**

_____

_____

_____

_____

# LEAD LIKE MOSES

---

*Moses answered the people, "Do not be afraid. Stand firm and you will see the deliverance the Lord will bring you today. The Egyptians you see today you will never see again. The Lord will fight for you; you need only to be still." –* Exodus 14:13-14

✤ **How can Moses tell them to not be afraid? Where does that assurance come from?**

_____

_____

_____

_____

_____

*Then the Lord said to Moses, "Why are you crying out to me? Tell the Israelites to move on" ... And when the Israelites saw the mighty hand of the Lord displayed against the Egyptians, the people feared the Lord and put their trust in him and in Moses his servant. –* Exodus 14:15, 31

Don't you love verse 15? Sometimes a leader has to tell people, "it's time to move on."

✤ **How does that apply to optimism?**

_____

_____

_____

# LEAD LIKE MOSES

_____

_____

✤ How do leaders get to the same results as found in verse 31?

_____

_____

_____

_____

_____

## Optimism Comes from Confidence in God's Faithfulness

_Then Moses summoned Joshua and said to him in the presence of all Israel, "Be strong and courageous, for you must go with this people into the land that the Lord swore to their ancestors to give them, and you must divide it among them as their inheritance. The Lord himself goes before you and will be with you; he will never leave you nor forsake you. Do not be afraid; do not be discouraged."_ – Deuteronomy 31:7-8

✤ If you internalized verse 8, how would that change your leadership?

_____

_____

# LEAD LIKE MOSES

_____

_____

_____

✤ **Does that mean you ignore reality?**

_____

_____

_____

_____

_____

As a Christ-follower, you have a great opportunity to make a positive difference in the lives of people all around you. In fact, you have a great responsibility to make a positive difference!

Imagine what our world would be like if we had leaders that called out the best we have to offer – who operated from a positive vision of what could be, rather than trying to scare us into action!

# LEAD LIKE MOSES

## CHAPTER FIVE: HAVING A COMPASS FOR CONFLICT

---

**Main Point**: Good leaders have a moral compass that guides them along.

If you happen to be human, you've had conflict. The key question for a leader is how you will handle conflict. That moment can make or break a leader. You will either gain credibility or lose it.

✤ **List leaders who handled conflict poorly and had their leadership weakened as a result:**

_____

_____

_____

_____

_____

## A Moral Compass

Crisis and conflict comes to everyone. It especially comes to those who seek to be leaders. Great leaders operate with a moral compass that is clear and grounded.

*When the people saw that Moses was so long in coming down from the mountain, they gathered around Aaron and said,*

# LEAD LIKE MOSES

*"Come, make us gods who will go before us. As for this fellow Moses who brought us up out of Egypt, we don't know what has happened to him." Aaron answered them, "Take off the gold earrings that your wives, your sons and your daughters are wearing, and bring them to me." So all the people took off their earrings and brought them to Aaron. He took what they handed him and made it into an idol cast in the shape of a calf, fashioning it with a tool. Then they said, "These are your gods, Israel, who brought you up out of Egypt." When Aaron saw this, he built an altar in front of the calf and announced, "Tomorrow there will be a festival to the Lord." So the next day the people rose early and sacrificed burnt offerings and presented fellowship offerings. Afterward they sat down to eat and drink and got up to indulge in revelry. Then the Lord said to Moses, "Go down, because your people, whom you brought up out of Egypt, have become corrupt. They have been quick to turn away from what I commanded them and have made themselves an idol cast in the shape of a calf. They have bowed down to it and sacrificed to it and have said, 'These are your gods, Israel, who brought you up out of Egypt.' "I have seen these people," the Lord said to Moses, "and they are a stiff-necked people. Now leave me alone so that my anger may burn against them and that I may destroy them. Then I will make you into a great nation." – Exodus 32:1-10*

✣ **What causes people (or teams) to be impatient?**

_____

_____

_____

_____

_____

# LEAD LIKE MOSES

✚ **How has a lack of patience affected a past leadership moment?**

_____

_____

_____

_____

_____

✚ **What temptation is Moses presented with in the last verse?**

_____

_____

_____

_____

_____

God expects leaders to take responsibility for the actions of people they lead (32:7). Although he had called Moses to this task, once Moses accepted the challenge, he became accountable for his leadership – including the present conflict.

_But Moses sought the favor of the Lord his God. "Lord," he said, "why should your anger burn against your people, whom you brought out of Egypt with great power and a mighty hand? Why should the Egyptians say, 'It was with evil intent that he brought_

# Lead Like Moses

*them out, to kill them in the mountains and to wipe them off the face of the earth'? Turn from your fierce anger; relent and do not bring disaster on your people. Remember your servants Abraham, Isaac and Israel, to whom you swore by your own self: 'I will make your descendants as numerous as the stars in the sky and I will give your descendants all this land I promised them, and it will be their inheritance forever.'" Then the Lord relented and did not bring on his people the disaster he had threatened.* – Exodus 32:11-14

✚ **In handling this conflict, to what does Moses appeal to?**

_____

_____

_____

_____

_____

*The next day Moses said to the people, "You have committed a great sin. But now I will go up to the Lord; perhaps I can make atonement for your sin." So Moses went back to the Lord and said, "Oh, what a great sin these people have committed! They have made themselves gods of gold. But now, please forgive their sin—but if not, then blot me out of the book you have written."* – Exodus 32:30-32

A leader without a moral compass would just shrug her shoulders and let it ride. Not Moses. As a Christ-follower, you have been given a moral compass – the example of Jesus.

# LEAD LIKE MOSES

✤ When it comes to conflict, what are your non-
negotiables that you will not compromise?

_____

_____

_____

_____

_____

_____

_____

_____

_____

_____

_____

_____

_____

# LEAD LIKE MOSES

## CHAPTER SIX: THE COMPASSION OF A LEADER

---

**Main Point**: Leaders must have concern for their followers.

In the Old Testament, compassion describes one aspect of God's covenantal relationship with his people. One of the Hebrew words translated "compassion" is derived from a root word meaning "womb," thus comparing God's love with maternal love. God's compassion, however, went beyond simply feeling the emotion; it was always demonstrated by definite acts that testified to his covenant with Israel. In spite of Israel's rebellions, God still had compassion on his people (2 Kgs 13:23; 2 Chr 36:15; Ps 78:38), as well as on all his creation (Ps 145:9). When Israel was chastised, the nation often feared that God had permanently withdrawn his favor (Ps 77:9; Is 27:11; 63:15; Jer 13:14; 21:7; Hos 13:14). Yet God's compassion would revive, and he would restore his people (Dt 30:3; Ps 135:14; Is 14:1; 49:13; 54:7–8; Jer 12:15; 30:18; Mi 7:19).

In the New Testament, Jesus Christ, the Son of God, exactly reflected the Father's compassion in his dealings with a fallen humanity. Jesus healed diseases and infirmities, cast out spirits, empowered others, and sent them out to do likewise. He fed hungry people and, in response to a mother's grief, raised her only son from the dead. Following Jesus' example, Christians are to show compassion in dealing with others. Jesus set forth the example in the parables of the Good Samaritan, who had compassion on a wounded traveler (Lk 10:33), and

# Lead Like Moses

the Prodigal Son, whose father had compassion on him when he returned home (15:20).[4]

For a leader to be a truly great leader, they must really care for the people they lead. This is what separates them from leaders who use people for selfish gain.

## The Softer Side of Moses

*When Pharaoh heard of this, he tried to kill Moses, but Moses fled from Pharaoh and went to live in Midian, where he sat down by a well. Now a priest of Midian had seven daughters, and they came to draw water and fill the troughs to water their father's flock. Some shepherds came along and drove them away, but Moses got up and came to their rescue and watered their flock. When the girls returned to Reuel their father, he asked them, "Why have you returned so early today?" They answered, "An Egyptian rescued us from the shepherds. He even drew water for us and watered the flock." "And where is he?" Reuel asked his daughters. "Why did you leave him? Invite him to have something to eat." – Exodus 2:15-20*

Moses has just fled Egypt, fearing for his life.

✚ **If you knew that Pharaoh wanted to have you killed, what would you be tempted to do?**

_____

_____

_____

---

[4] Elwell, Walter A., and Philip Wesley Comfort. *Tyndale Bible dictionary* 2001 : 306. Print. Tyndale Reference Library.

# LEAD LIKE MOSES

_____

_____

✤ **What does story tell us about Moses?**

_____

_____

_____

_____

## The Example of God

_The Lord said, "I have indeed seen the misery of my people in Egypt. I have heard them crying out because of their slave drivers, and I am concerned about their suffering. So I have come down to rescue them from the hand of the Egyptians and to bring them up out of that land into a good and spacious land, a land flowing with milk and honey—the home of the Canaanites, Hittites, Amorites, Perizzites, Hivites and Jebusites. – Exodus 3:7-8_

The suffering of his people touched God's heart. If Moses was going to carry out the mission given to him, he had to share the pain that was in the heart of God.

True leadership is impossible without compassion for the captivity and suffering of those who are to be led.

_The next day Moses said to the people, "You have committed a great sin. But now I will go up to the Lord; perhaps I can make_

# LEAD LIKE MOSES

*atonement for your sin." So Moses went back to the Lord and said, "Oh, what a great sin these people have committed! They have made themselves gods of gold. But now, please forgive their sin—but if not, then blot me out of the book you have written." –* Exodus 32:30–32

After the building of the golden calf, we see the full depth of Moses' compassionate identification with the people when he interceded with God to forgive their sin and even offered himself to be blotted out of God's book to make atonement for them.

✚ **How is Moses able to do this?**

_____

_____

_____

_____

_____

## Servant or Self-Serving

A godly leader cares more about the good of the group than he does his own enrichment.

*The word of the Lord came to me: "Son of man, prophesy against the shepherds of Israel; prophesy and say to them: 'This is what the Sovereign Lord says: Woe to you shepherds of Israel who only take care of yourselves! Should not shepherds take care of the flock? You eat the curds, clothe yourselves with the wool and slaughter the choice animals, but you do not take care of the flock. You have not strengthened the weak or healed the sick or*

# Lead Like Moses

*bound up the injured. You have not brought back the strays or searched for the lost. You have ruled them harshly and brutally. So they were scattered because there was no shepherd, and when they were scattered they became food for all the wild animals. My sheep wandered over all the mountains and on every high hill. They were scattered over the whole earth, and no one searched or looked for them. 'Therefore, you shepherds, hear the word of the Lord: As surely as I live, declares the Sovereign Lord, because my flock lacks a shepherd and so has been plundered and has become food for all the wild animals, and because my shepherds did not search for my flock but cared for themselves rather than for my flock, therefore, you shepherds, hear the word of the Lord: This is what the Sovereign Lord says: I am against the shepherds and will hold them accountable for my flock. I will remove them from tending the flock so that the shepherds can no longer feed themselves. I will rescue my flock from their mouths, and it will no longer be food for them. " 'For this is what the Sovereign Lord says: I myself will search for my sheep and look after them. As a shepherd looks after his scattered flock when he is with them, so will I look after my sheep. I will rescue them from all the places where they were scattered on a day of clouds and darkness. I will bring them out from the nations and gather them from the countries, and I will bring them into their own land. I will pasture them on the mountains of Israel, in the ravines and in all the settlements in the land. I will tend them in a good pasture, and the mountain heights of Israel will be their grazing land. There they will lie down in good grazing land, and there they will feed in a rich pasture on the mountains of Israel. I myself will tend my sheep and have them lie down, declares the Sovereign Lord. I will search for the lost and bring back the strays. I will bind up the injured and strengthen the weak, but the sleek and the strong I will destroy. I will shepherd the flock with justice. – Ezekiel 34:1-16*

# LEAD LIKE MOSES

✤ **What are the characteristics of good shepherds?**

_____

_____

_____

_____

_____

✤ **How would seeing yourself as a shepherd change the way you lead?**

_____

_____

_____

_____

_____

Shepherding was the way of Jesus ... John 10:1-18

# LEAD LIKE MOSES

## The Prayer of a Compassionate Leader

*Moses bowed to the ground at once and worshiped. "Lord," he said, "if I have found favor in your eyes, then let the Lord go with us. Although this is a stiff-necked people, forgive our wickedness and our sin, and take us as your inheritance." –* Exodus 34:8-9

✤ **What is your prayer for the people you are currently leading?**

_____

_____

_____

_____

_____

_____

_____

_____

_____

# LEAD LIKE MOSES
## CHAPTER SEVEN: LISTENING TO GOD

---

**Main Point**: Godly leaders listen to guidance from God.

One consistent characteristic of Moses is that he received guidance from God. The times when he chose to ignore or not seek God's guidance often ended in disaster.

## Examples of a Listening Ear

### Exodus 3

*There the angel of the Lord appeared to him in flames of fire from within a bush. Moses saw that though the bush was on fire it did not burn up. So Moses thought, "I will go over and see this strange sight—why the bush does not burn up." ... But Moses said to God, "Who am I that I should go to Pharaoh and bring the Israelites out of Egypt?" And God said, "I will be with you. And this will be the sign to you that it is I who have sent you: When you have brought the people out of Egypt, you will worship God on this mountain." ... "Go, assemble the elders of Israel and say to them, 'The Lord, the God of your fathers—the God of Abraham, Isaac and Jacob—appeared to me and said: I have watched over you and have seen what has been done to you in Egypt. ... "The elders of Israel will listen to you. Then you and the elders are to go to the king of Egypt and say to him, 'The Lord, the God of the Hebrews, has met with us. Let us take a three-day journey into the wilderness to offer sacrifices to the Lord our God.'"*

# LEAD LIKE MOSES

**Exodus 4**

*Moses answered, "What if they do not believe me or listen to me and say, 'The Lord did not appear to you'?" ... Then the Lord said, "If they do not believe you or pay attention to the first sign, they may believe the second. But if they do not believe these two signs or listen to you, take some water from the Nile and pour it on the dry ground. The water you take from the river will become blood on the ground." ... But Moses said, "Pardon your servant, Lord. Please send someone else." Then the Lord's anger burned against Moses and he said, "What about your brother, Aaron the Levite? I know he can speak well. He is already on his way to meet you, and he will be glad to see you. You shall speak to him and put words in his mouth; I will help both of you speak and will teach you what to do. He will speak to the people for you, and it will be as if he were your mouth and as if you were God to him. But take this staff in your hand so you can perform the signs with it." ... Then Moses told Aaron everything the Lord had sent him to say, and also about all the signs he had commanded him to perform. Moses and Aaron brought together all the elders of the Israelites, and Aaron told them everything the Lord had said to Moses. He also performed the signs before the people, and they believed. And when they heard that the Lord was concerned about them and had seen their misery, they bowed down and worshiped.*

**Exodus 19**

*Then Moses went up to God, and the Lord called to him from the mountain and said, "This is what you are to say to the descendants of Jacob and what you are to tell the people of Israel ... These are the words you are to speak to the Israelites." ... So Moses went back and summoned the elders of the people and set before them all the words the Lord had commanded him to speak. The people all responded together, "We will do everything the Lord has said." So Moses brought their answer back to*

# LEAD LIKE MOSES

*the Lord. The Lord said to Moses, "I am going to come to you in a dense cloud, so that the people will hear me speaking with you and will always put their trust in you." Then Moses told the Lord what the people had said … After Moses had gone down the mountain to the people, he consecrated them, and they washed their clothes … As the sound of the trumpet grew louder and louder, Moses spoke and the voice of God answered him.*

*The Lord descended to the top of Mount Sinai and called Moses to the top of the mountain. So Moses went up and the Lord said to him, "Go down and warn the people so they do not force their way through to see the Lord and many of them perish … So Moses went down to the people and told them.*

✚ **Based on these passages, how would you characterize the relationship between God and Moses?**

_____

_____

_____

_____

_____

# LEAD LIKE MOSES
## Posture and Character

In this Marc Chagall painting, we see Moses reaching up to receive the Ten Commandments from God. This posture defines his character. Moses is not portrayed in the Bible as a decisive strategist, a resourceful analyst, or a great military leader. Rather, he was the faithful recipient and teacher of God's word.

✤ **As a leader, what are you doing to "reach up" to God?**

_____

_____

# LEAD LIKE MOSES

_____

_____

_____

✤ **What keeps people from "reaching up" to God?**

_____

_____

_____

_____

## The Evidence of a Listening Relationship

*Miriam and Aaron began to talk against Moses because of his
Cushite wife, for he had married a Cushite. "Has the Lord spoken
only through Moses?" they asked. "Hasn't he also spoken through
us?" And the Lord heard this. (Now Moses was a very humble
man, more humble than anyone else on the face of the earth.) At
once the Lord said to Moses, Aaron and Miriam, "Come out to the
tent of meeting, all three of you." So the three of them went out.
Then the Lord came down in a pillar of cloud; he stood at the
entrance to the tent and summoned Aaron and Miriam. When
the two of them stepped forward, he said, "Listen to my words:
"When there is a prophet among you, I, the Lord, reveal myself to
them in visions, I speak to them in dreams. But this is not true of
my servant Moses; he is faithful in all my house. With him I speak
face to face, clearly and not in riddles; he sees the form of
the Lord. Why then were you not afraid to speak against my
servant Moses?" – Numbers 12:1–8*

# LEAD LIKE MOSES

✤ **What made Moses different from other prophets/leaders?**

_____

_____

_____

_____

_____

*Since then, no prophet has risen in Israel like Moses, whom the Lord knew face to face, who did all those signs and wonders the Lord sent him to do in Egypt—to Pharaoh and to all his officials and to his whole land. For no one has ever shown the mighty power or performed the awesome deeds that Moses did in the sight of all Israel. – Deuteronomy 34:10-12*

✤ **What can you do to improve your divine listening skills?**

_____

_____

_____

_____

_____

# Lead Like Moses
## Chapter Eight: Leaders Develop Leaders

---

**Main Point**: Effective leaders will raise up the next generation of leaders.

"Success without a successor is failure." – Warren Webster

One of the primary responsibilities of leadership is to not only lead but to train others to lead as well. Training and mentoring others is not easy; it's one reason why many leaders never become leaders of leaders.

# LEAD LIKE MOSES

## Even the Greatest Leaders Never Finish the Work

God called Moses to a very specific task: to lead God's people to the Promised Land. But Moses will not be the one to complete the task – that would be left to his successor.

*The nations you will dispossess listen to those who practice sorcery or divination. But as for you, the Lord your God has not permitted you to do so. The Lord your God will raise up for you a prophet like me from among you, from your fellow Israelites. You must listen to him. For this is what you asked of the Lord your God at Horeb on the day of the assembly when you said, "Let us not hear the voice of the Lord our God nor see this great fire anymore, or we will die." The Lord said to me: "What they say is good. I will raise up for them a prophet like you from among their fellow Israelites, and I will put my words in his mouth. He will tell them everything I command him. I myself will call to account anyone who does not listen to my words that the prophet speaks in my name. – Deuteronomy 18:15–19*

This passage points out a very important aspect of spiritual leadership: God is the one who raises up leaders. Our responsibility is to recognize those that God has given the gift of leadership.

*Then Moses went out and spoke these words to all Israel: "I am now a hundred and twenty years old and I am no longer able to lead you. The Lord has said to me, 'You shall not cross the Jordan.' The Lord your God himself will cross over ahead of you. He will destroy these nations before you, and you will take possession of their land. Joshua also will cross over ahead of you, as the Lord said. And the Lord will do to them what he did to Sihon and Og, the kings of the Amorites, whom he destroyed along with their land. The Lord will deliver them to you, and you must do to them all that I have commanded you. Be strong and*

# LEAD LIKE MOSES

*courageous. Do not be afraid or terrified because of them, for the Lord your God goes with you; he will never leave you nor forsake you." Then Moses summoned Joshua and said to him in the presence of all Israel, "Be strong and courageous, for you must go with this people into the land that the Lord swore to their ancestors to give them, and you must divide it among them as their inheritance. The Lord himself goes before you and will be with you; he will never leave you nor forsake you. Do not be afraid; do not be discouraged."* – Deuteronomy 31:1–8

✤ **In every leadership transition, what is the one constant?**

_____

_____

_____

_____

_____

✤ **Why would Moses address Joshua in front of all the people?**

_____

_____

_____

_____

_____

# LEAD LIKE MOSES

*And Moses the servant of the Lord died there in Moab, as the Lord had said. He buried him in Moab, in the valley opposite Beth Peor, but to this day no one knows where his grave is. Moses was a hundred and twenty years old when he died, yet his eyes were not weak nor his strength gone. The Israelites grieved for Moses in the plains of Moab thirty days, until the time of weeping and mourning was over. Now Joshua son of Nun was filled with the spirit of wisdom because Moses had laid his hands on him. So the Israelites listened to him and did what the Lord had commanded Moses. – Deuteronomy 34:5-9*

An important part of the responsibility of leadership is to identify and raise up the next generation of leaders to follow.

✜ **Joshua "interned" with Moses for 40 years. If a person refuses to serve, submit and follow another leader, how can they ask anyone to follow or take instructions from them?**

_____

_____

_____

_____

_____

## Empowering the Next Generation

Put yourself in Moses' shoes for a minute: Moses is asked to commission the person who would achieve what Moses had spent 40 years trying to achieve – reach the Promised Land. Although he might have been tempted to be bitter, he chose to end well.

# LEAD LIKE MOSES

*The Israelites had done all the work just as the Lord had commanded Moses. Moses inspected the work and saw that they had done it just as the Lord had commanded. So Moses blessed them.* – Exodus 39:43

✤ **What important leadership trait does Moses exhibit in this passage?**

_____

_____

_____

_____

*So the Lord said to Moses, "Take Joshua son of Nun, a man in whom is the spirit of leadership, and lay your hand on him. Have him stand before Eleazar the priest and the entire assembly and commission him in their presence. Give him some of your authority so the whole Israelite community will obey him. –* Numbers 27:18-20

✤ **How does a leader give away some of their authority?**

_____

_____

_____

_____

# LEAD LIKE MOSES

✤ **Why is this important when it comes to leadership development?**

_____

_____

_____

_____

## Six Things Moses Did to Raise Up Joshua

1. He believed in Joshua
2. He mentored Joshua
3. He prayed for Joshua
4. He empowered Joshua
5. He publicly supported Joshua
6. He allowed Joshua to lead

✤ **Which of these do you struggle with the most?**

_____

_____

_____

_____

_____

# LEAD LIKE MOSES
## CHAPTER NINE: LEADERS LISTEN TO OTHERS

---

**Main Point**: A good leader cannot be stubborn.

Refusing to take advice and being determined to follow a failing course of action are not signs of good leadership.

✤ **What are they signs of?**

_____

_____

_____

_____

_____

# The Problem

Perhaps because he took the call of God so seriously, Moses began his leadership career as a workaholic.

_Now Jethro, the priest of Midian and father-in-law of Moses, heard of everything God had done for Moses and for his people Israel, and how the Lord had brought Israel out of Egypt ... Jethro, Moses' father-in-law, together with Moses' sons and wife, came to him in the wilderness, where he was camped near the mountain of God. ... Moses told his father-in-law about everything the Lord had done to Pharaoh and the Egyptians for Israel's sake and about all the hardships they had met along the_

# LEAD LIKE MOSES

*way and how the Lord had saved them. Jethro was delighted to hear about all the good things the Lord had done for Israel in rescuing them from the hand of the Egyptians ... The next day Moses took his seat to serve as judge for the people, and they stood around him from morning till evening. When his father-in-law saw all that Moses was doing for the people, he said, "What is this you are doing for the people? Why do you alone sit as judge, while all these people stand around you from morning till evening?" Moses answered him, "Because the people come to me to seek God's will. Whenever they have a dispute, it is brought to me, and I decide between the parties and inform them of God's decrees and instructions." Moses' father-in-law replied, "What you are doing is not good. You and these people who come to you will only wear yourselves out. The work is too heavy for you; you cannot handle it alone. Listen now to me and I will give you some advice, and may God be with you. You must be the people's representative before God and bring their disputes to him. Teach them his decrees and instructions, and show them the way they are to live and how they are to behave. But select capable men from all the people—men who fear God, trustworthy men who hate dishonest gain—and appoint them as officials over thousands, hundreds, fifties and tens. Have them serve as judges for the people at all times, but have them bring every difficult case to you; the simple cases they can decide themselves. That will make your load lighter, because they will share it with you. If you do this and God so commands, you will be able to stand the strain, and all these people will go home satisfied." Moses listened to his father-in-law and did everything he said. – Exodus 18*

Moses had good intentions but he wasn't being wise. Instead, he was working himself to death – and depriving other leaders from exercising their leadership.

# Lead Like Moses

✤ **What was Moses relying on?**

_____

_____

_____

_____

_____

✤ **What could Moses have said to Jethro?**

_____

_____

_____

_____

_____

Moses listened to his father-in-law when Jethro had a better idea. A good leader is more concerned with getting the best ideas rather than needing to create all the ideas. Those who must create all the ideas become bottlenecks for growth and are susceptible to burnout.

✤ **What can you do to improve your ability to listen to others?**

_____

_____

# LEAD LIKE MOSES

_____

_____

_____

## Spread the Load

Teams make better decisions than individuals and effective leaders will rely on the input from others.

The benefits of team include:

1. Teams are more likely to succeed (Exodus 17:10-13)
2. Leaders are less likely to burn out (Exodus 18:17-18, 23)
3. You will do better work (Numbers 11:16-17)
4. You will ensure continuity (Ecclesiastes 2:17-19)

5. _____

6. _____

7. _____

8. _____

9. _____

10. _____

# LEAD LIKE MOSES

## CHAPTER TEN: LEADERS KEEP GOING

---

**Main Point**: A good leader never quits too soon.

Walt Disney was fired from a newspaper job because he "lacked imagination and had no original ideas."

Lee Iaccoca was a rising star at Ford Motor Company until he clashed with Henry Ford, Jr. He was eventually let go and later became the CEO of Chrysler.

Elvis Presley was once told by the concert manager of the Grand Old Opry that he would be better off going back to driving trucks for a career.

## Facing Discouragement

*Moses heard the people of every family wailing at the entrance to their tents. The Lord became exceedingly angry, and Moses was troubled. He asked the Lord, "Why have you brought this trouble on your servant? What have I done to displease you that you put the burden of all these people on me? Did I conceive all these people? Did I give them birth? Why do you tell me to carry them in my arms, as a nurse carries an infant, to the land you promised on oath to their ancestors? Where can I get meat for all these people? They keep wailing to me, 'Give us meat to eat!' I cannot carry all these people by myself; the burden is too heavy for me. If this is how you are going to treat me, please go ahead and kill me—if I have found favor in your eyes—and do not let me face my own ruin."* – Numbers 11:10-15

# LEAD LIKE MOSES

✤ Have the people you've led ever made you feel this way?

_____

_____

_____

_____

_____

✤ What are common sources of discouragement? Which sources might be unique to leadership?

_____

_____

_____

_____

_____

Here is a key point to remember: When everyone else has given up, it is the responsibility of a leader to keep hope alive.

## Motivation Comes from a Higher Source

_By faith Moses, when he had grown up, refused to be known as the son of Pharaoh's daughter. He chose to be mistreated along with the people of God rather than to enjoy the fleeting pleasures of sin. He regarded disgrace for the sake of Christ as of greater value than the treasures of Egypt, because he was looking ahead to his reward._ – Hebrews 11:24-26

# LEAD LIKE MOSES

✤ **Why do leaders put up with discouragement?**

_____

_____

_____

_____

_____

*Since then, no prophet has risen in Israel like Moses, whom the Lord knew face to face, who did all those signs and wonders the Lord sent him to do in Egypt—to Pharaoh and to all his officials and to his whole land. For no one has ever shown the mighty power or performed the awesome deeds that Moses did in the sight of all Israel.* – Deuteronomy 34:10-12

The motivation to lead must be drawn from a great cause. Through all of the desert years, Moses kept God – and his mission – in mind.

✤ **What great cause are you involved in?**

_____

_____

_____

_____

_____

# LEAD LIKE MOSES

✢ If you don't have a great cause, how will you find one?

_____

_____

_____

_____

_____

_____

_____

_____

_____

_____

_____

_____

# LEAD LIKE MOSES

## A Prayer of Moses, A Man of God (Psalm 90)

*Lord, you have been our dwelling place throughout all generations. Before the mountains were born or you brought forth the earth and the world, from everlasting to everlasting you are God. You turn men back to dust, saying, "Return to dust, O sons of men." For a thousand years in your sight are like a day that has just gone by, or like a watch in the night. You sweep men away in the sleep of death; they are like the new grass of the morning — though in the morning it springs up new, by evening it is dry and withered. We are consumed by your anger and terrified by your indignation. You have set our iniquities before you, our secret sins in the light of your presence. All our days pass away under your wrath; we finish our years with a moan. The length of our days is seventy years — or eighty, if we have the strength; yet their span is but trouble and sorrow, for they quickly pass, and we fly away. Who knows the power of your anger? For your wrath is as great as the fear that is due you. Teach us to number our days aright, that we may gain a heart of wisdom. Relent, O Lord! How long will it be? Have compassion on your servants. Satisfy us in the morning with your unfailing love, that we may sing for joy and be glad all our days. Make us glad for as many days as you have afflicted us, for as many years as we have seen trouble. May your deeds be shown to your servants, your splendor to their children. May the favor of the Lord our God rest upon us; establish the work of our hands for us — yes, establish the work of our hands.*

# Lead Like Moses
## About the Author

Ken Hensley was born and raised in Peoria, Ill. (the home of Caterpillar Tractors) and did his undergraduate work at Freed-Hardeman University and graduate work at Bethel Theological Seminary. He married his college sweetheart (Tonya) and both have been blessed with two wonderful daughters, Hannah and Hope. Tonya is a teacher at Southeast Christian School in Parker.

The Lord has blessed Ken and his family with the opportunity to lead churches in several of America's finest cities — San Diego, San Francisco, Atlanta, and now Denver.

In 1999, Ken entered the dot com world and co-founded a business that enabled non-profits to make better use of emerging technologies. During this same time, he also worked in the pre-launch days at Christianity.com — the days when the coffee and donuts were still available for free and foosball breaks were required.

In the spring of 2004, Ken decided to pursue the call God had placed on his heart to start churches that would fit new and emerging generations. In 2005, Ken was hired by Stadia: New Church Strategies to return to San Diego and start LifePoint Christian Church. During his four years with LifePoint Ken had the pleasure of seeing people who were disconnected from God

# LEAD LIKE MOSES

find their way back to him. Ken also had the privilege of partnering with other new churches to reach San Diego and beyond.

Ken and his family relocated from San Diego to south Denver, where he serves as the Senior Pastor at Mountainview Christian Church in Highlands Ranch. He also serves on the Board of Directors for Church Planters of the Rockies, an organization that starts new churches along the Front Range of Colorado.

# LEAD LIKE MOSES

## ✤ Get in Touch with Ken

Twitter: @kenhensley
Facebook: facebook.com/kenhensley
Blog: www.kenhensley.com